I0390782

Cyber Incident and Crisis Management
In organizations and companies

Dr. Ishai Dror

Israel, March 2019

Cyberattacks have already become common phenomena and are expected to accompany us into the foreseeable future. This is a new form of warfare and crime, its nature and potency likely to change in parallel to ongoing developments in technology.

Our intent is not to spread fear. Rather, it is to enhance managers' awareness to the dangers of cyberattacks, to illustrate their possible impacts on companies and organizations, and to present some managerial approaches for coping with them.

Focusing on the management of Cyber events and crises, the purpose of this guide is to serve as a supporting tool for managers: Board members, senior managers, business units' managers, IT managers and Cyber Security managers in large and medium sized companies and organizations.

As a document aimed at managers, it is less concerned with the technological aspects, but focuses mainly on the managerial and organizational aspects.

Dr. Ishai Dror consults to large companies and organizations and has managed large scale managerial exercises in Crisis Management, Business Continuity and Cybersecurity Management. He has served as a consultant at the Israel National Cyber Directorate and for the World Bank (seminars and exercises for managements in various countries).
He teaches a unique Crisis Management course in academic graduate programs.

Cyber - an abbreviation of Cybernetics.

Cybernetics - The term Cybernetics stems from the Greek κυβερνήτης (Cybernétēs), meaning steersman or governor – a captain.

The term got fame following Norbert Wiener's book *Cybernetics* (1948).

According to Wiener, "The purpose of Cybernetics is to develop a language and techniques that will enable us indeed to attack the problem of control and communication."

Cyber Security Incident -

UK NCSC defines a Cyber security incident as:
- A breach of a system's security policy in order to affect its integrity or availability
- The unauthorised access or attempted access to a system

The NCSC defines a significant cyber security incident as one which may have:
- The potential to cause major impact to the continued operation of an organisation

A Significant Cyber Security Incident -
- Not only the breach or the unauthorized access – **but also their (potential) organizational and business impacts**:
  - Unauthorized use or manipulation of data, money theft, damage to (data) assets, disruptions in operation and services, business damage, damage to reputation, etc.
- Blurring boundaries between Cyber incidents / frauds and embezzlements / theft / damage to assets / espionage / manipulation.

Global Cybersecurity Threat Landscape

Overt and covert threats

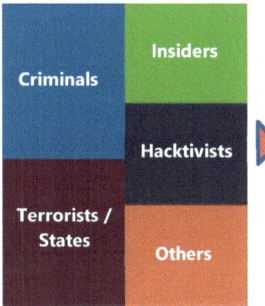

Publicly-Known Attacks

Non-Public
Cyberattacks yet to be discovered, reported, or within the classified domain

Hostile Actors

- Criminals
- Insiders
- Hacktivists
- Terrorists / States
- Others

Vulnerabilities

- Hyper-Interconnectivity of information systems
- Rapid Technological Infrastructure Expansion
- Hard to Define Organizational Perimeters
- Lack of experienced professionals
- Lack of synchronization in cross-organizational control processes
- Organizational awareness

Risks

- Information Manipulation
- Intellectual Property Theft
- Financial losses
- Operational Disruptions
- Negative Media Publicity
- Lawsuits
- Loss of Public Confidence

Based on Booz Allen Hamilton Inc.

Cyberattacks can have impacts in various levels:

Levels of Impacts

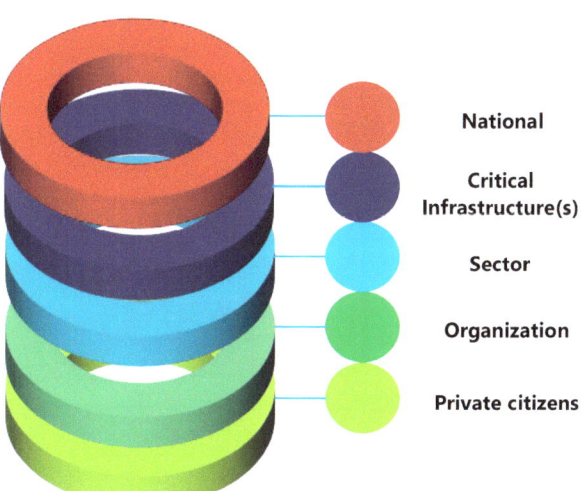

- National
- Critical Infrastructure(s)
- Sector
- Organization
- Private citizens

The focus of this guide is the organizational level.

2. Cyberattacks - Trends

Cyberattacks are undergoing a process of **Globalization**: From anywhere to everywhere.	The Wannacry ransomware attack in 2017 provides a good example: Computers in dozens of countries and organizations around the world were attacked simultaneously.

The globalization of Cyberattacks -

The 'Wannacry' ransomware attack
The attack has hit more than 200,000 victims in at least 150 countries, says Europol

UK	The National Health Service
Spain	Telefonica
France	Renault
Germany	Deutsche Bahn
US	FedEx
Russia	Central Bank, M. of Interior
Brazil	Petrobras
Japan	Several city offices

© AFP

No critical sector escapes the Cyber threat -

November 2016
NHS hospitals
Hospital machines were frozen to demand ransom cash; at least four NHS (National Health Service) funds were attacked

November 2016
Yahoo
Data breach of 1 billion accounts

December 2015 & December 2016
Power grid in Ukraine
230,000 people were left without power for up to 6 hours; first time that a cyber-weapon was successfully used against a nation's power grid

November 2016
Tesco Bank
Around £2.5 million was stolen from around 9,000 customers in this hack, the largest on a UK bank

February 2016
Central bank of Bangladesh
USD 81 million were lost and a further USD 850 million in transactions were prevented from being processed

November 2016
Deutsche Telekom
900,000 (or about 4.5 percent of its 20 million fixed-line customers) suffered internet outages over two days

February 2016
FBI and Homeland Security
Personal details of over 20,000 employees of the Federal Bureau of Investigation and 9,000 of the Department of Homeland Security were accessed

October 2016
Australian Red Cross
Personal data of 550,000 blood donators stolen

April 2016
Philippines' Commission on Elections (COMELEC)
Personal information of every single voter in the Philippines — approx. 55 million people — was compromised by Anonymous

Pie chart sectors: Democratic institutions, Financial services, Energy, Security, Health, Communication, IT Services

October 2016
Domain name provider Dyn
A distributed denial of service attack resulted in the break-down of some of the biggest websites in the world including Twitter, The Guardian, Netflix, Reddit, Airbnb and CNN

April 2016
Democratic National Committee
Publication of 20,000 e-mails stolen from the Democratic National Committee

European Political Strategy Centre

It happens to the of best us... and to many others who keep it a secret

Banks

J.P.Morgan

Energy

Ukraine Power Grid

Oil Companies Get Hacked in Massive Cyberattack in Norway

Social

Quora

Health

Shipping

Port de Barcelona

Port of Antwerp

Professional Services

Aviation

Commerce

Government

Equifax

Equifax's stock price after 2017 Sept. 7's hacking announcement

- A top credit bureau
- Personal and financial data leakage of 147.9 million people
- Investigations by federal and state-level authorities, including US Congress, FTC, SEC, FBI, and regulators in Canada and UK
- CIO and CSO "retired", CEO "resigned"
- Class-action lawsuits in an unknown volume
- Cost estimates – over $600 million (including systems upgrade, customer care and direct and indirect costs)

The attack

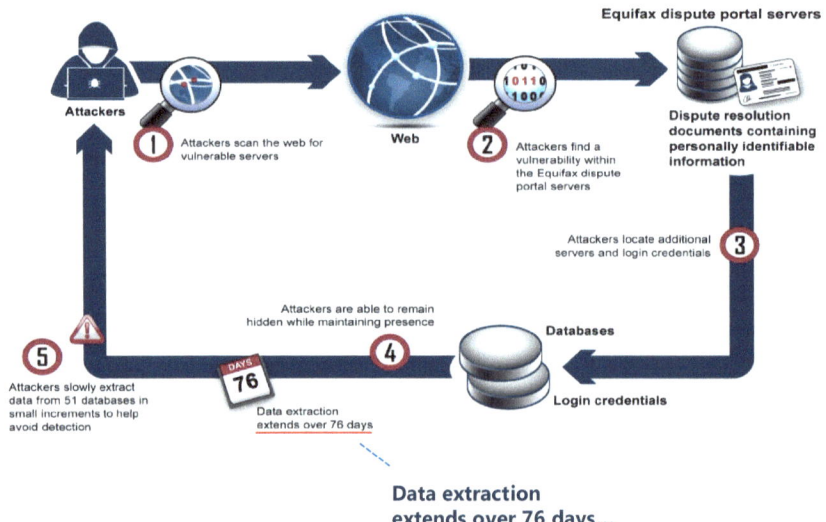

Data extraction extends over 76 days...

Source: GAO, based on information provided by Equifax.   GAO-18-559

3. Cyber Crisis Management - Guiding Principles

The Cyber Crisis - character traits -

A Cyber crisis is a crisis that there is a reasonable basis to assume is caused by a cyberattack.

A Cyber crisis may occur as a stand-alone event or during a national emergency (war, earthquake, etc.).

In times of national emergency or tension, cyberattack efforts may increase, resulting in a greater risk for Cyber crisis.

Possible impacts -

The challenges for the organization during a Cyber crisis are not just technological. They may be expressed in a wide range of organizational, functional and business aspects:

Possible impacts of Cyber incidents

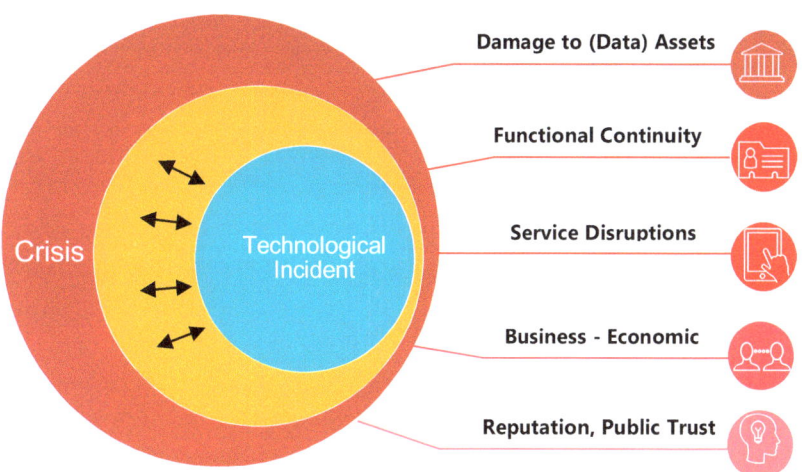

In practice, then, a Cyber crisis has two layers:

- **Causes** - The technological aspects related to the cyberattack and their direct effects on Cyber assets.
- **Impacts** - The wider implications in the internal and external organizational environment.

The Responsibility of the Senior Management -

In view of the fact that the impacts of a Cyber crisis may manifest in a wide range of organizational, functional and business aspects, the management of a Cyber crisis, and the preparations for it, are the responsibility of the senior echelon of the organization - the board of directors and senior management - and not only of the professional-technological level.

However, despite the growing awareness of the Cyber threat, many senior executives are unaware of their role in Cyber Security in general, and during a significant Cyber security incident in particular:

"Senior managers in most businesses and charities prioritise Cyber security, but this is still not always matched by action or engagement from senior management teams."

The Crisis Management Goals -

1) Minimize the functional, business-financial and reputational damage
2) Safeguard data assets, with emphasis on information assets that are sensitive or vital for functional continuity
3) Prevent further damage to infrastructures and other systems
4) Continue to provide services to the public/customers the best you can, with emphasis on **essential services**
5) Comply with the requirements of law and regulation
6) Make all efforts to neutralize the incident's causes as quick as possible

Crisis Management - supporting principles -

- **Reporting and escalation** - Reporting and updating processes "up and crosswise"
- **Centralizing decision-making** and elevating the level of decision makers - Crisis management team (CMT)
- **Sense making** - the quick establishment of a meaningful and clearest possible Situation Snapshot for the decision makers - CSIRT
- **Internal coordination** - with emphasis on the coordination between the techno-operational and the business units
- **Effective communication** with external stakeholders - customers, suppliers, the media, authorities
- **Proactivity** – proactive, "forward-looking" thinking

The Cyber Crisis Life Cycle -

Each crisis has its own unique "life cycle": Some of the crises are "exploding" crises, they come abruptly and their implications for the organization and its activities are immediately apparent, while others are "build" crises, that is, a gradual process of escalation takes place in their intensity and ramifications.

A schematic "life cycle" of a Cyber crisis looks like this:

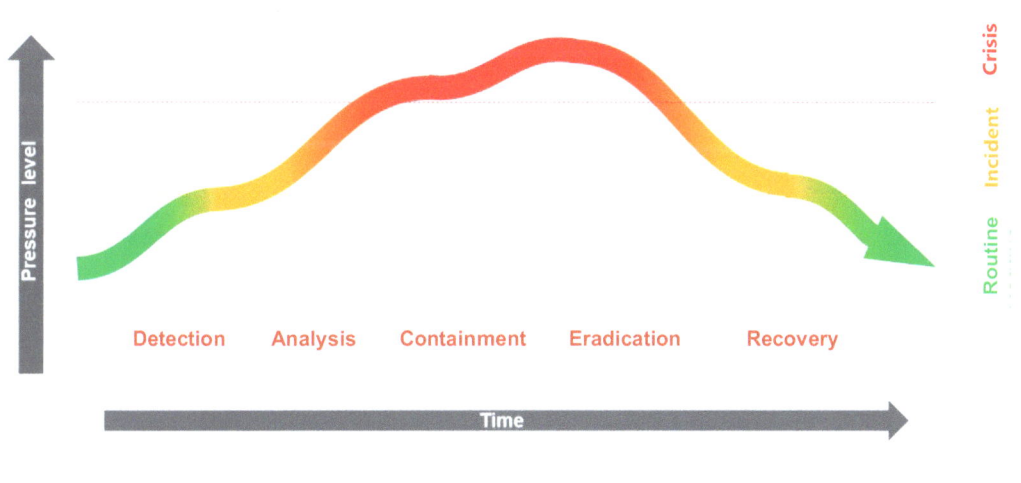

The Cyber crisis life cycle

Detection   Analysis   Containment   Eradication   Recovery

Based on ENISA

Environmental challenges during a crisis -

Organizational challenges
Disagreements, behaviors, feelings

Political challenges
Power struggles, conflicts, pressures

Crisis management:
- Teams' activation
- Situation assessments
- Decision making and formulation of strategies
- Response (actions)

Business challenges
Business continuity, Customers, market

Media challenges
Exposure, rumors, slander

Cyber Incident Severity Levels -

The Severity Levels of a significant Cyber incident determine the severity of the situation resulting from the cyberattack (or suspected cyberattack) and serve as a basis for activating a suitable action plan in response to that situation.

The formal decision on a specific severity level, or a change in the severity level, is called **declaration on a severity level.**

Such declaration is the authority of the senior authorized rank on the national, sectoral or organizational level.

In cases in which a Cyber Incident severity level has not been declared by an authorized authority (on the national or sectoral levels), and there are grounds to suspect the development of a crisis in a certain organization, the senior echelon of the organization is supposed to declare a suitable level of severity for the organization.

An organization may define a higher severity level than defined by national or sectoral authorities, but not a lower one (only in exceptional cases).

National and Security authorities often tend to define a rather complex scale of severity levels. Experience shows that companies and organizations distance themselves from guidelines that are too complex.
If regulation does not demand a specific scale of severity levels, it is recommended to implement a clear and simple scale, such as the one presented below.

Cyber Incident Severity Levels

Ongoing protection against attacks	**Routine**	Ongoing protection of the organizational systems and services, using technological tools and organizational controls
Warnings of a significant attack; no attack yet	**Alert (Readiness)**	Alert by national/sectoral authorities; cyberattack in other (relevant) organizations; reports of relevant attacks abroad
Severity Levels upon occurrence of a significant attack	**Level 1**	Intrusion to organization's assets without substantial functional or business damage; limited damage to information or data; an attack that may have operative significance but can reasonably be contained within a relatively short time
	Level 2	Significant damage to organizational assets; theft of sensitive information; significant fraud and theft of money; significant damage to operational or business capabilities; potential damage to reputation

4. Cyber Crisis Management – The Organizational Setup

General -

The organizational response is expected to deal with threats and challenges **on two levels**:

- Coping with the **Incident causes** (mostly technological)
- Coping with the **Incident impacts** (organizational, operational, business and reputational aspects)

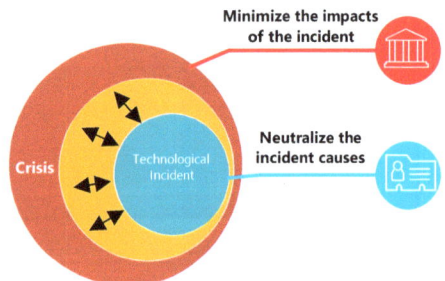

Main designated teams -

These two levels also define the main designated Crisis Management teams:

- **CSIRT** - **Computer Security Incident Response Team** - the role of this professional level team is to cope with the technological aspects of the Cyber incident, to operate the capabilities necessary to deal with the cyberattack, and to professionally lead the process of recovery from its damage.
- **CMT** - **Crisis Management Team** - the organization's senior managerial team, responsible for decision-making at the organizational level and for managing the crisis as a whole in its organizational, operational, business and reputational aspects.

Cyber Crisis Management - Main designated teams

Board

CEO

Crisis Management Team
- General Management
- Situational awareness meetings
- Strategies and directions
- Business decisions
- stakeholders' management

Managerial decision-making

- Responsibility
- Guidance on essential-strategic aspects

- Led by the CEO (or his/her second)
- Senior Managers (VP's)
- Key professional experts (invitees)

CSIRT
- Intelligence & Information
- Sense Making
- Detection & Analysis
- Coordination with external professional teams
- Containment & Recovery

Professional-technological response

- Led by the professional manager responsible for Cyber security
- SOC and information security representatives
- Relevant IT professionals
- Representatives from relevant BUs
- External consultants and Incident Response experts

Roles of the Crisis Management Team -

- Decide on the Cyber Incident Severity Level
- Formulate action guidelines - in accordance with the relevant authorities' instructions
- Guide the CSIRT team and receive updates from it
- Provide instructions with respect to customers and other stakeholders
- Define business and financial guidelines (as necessary)
- Set the strategy vis-à-vis the media (traditional and social media)
- Provide guidelines with respect to the coordination with relevant Authorities

- Continuous management of the crisis through periodic Situation assessments
- Follow-up on the execution of the response activities

Roles of the CSIRT -

Crisis Management team

Relevant external professional bodies **Reporting, updating and consulting** **Internal professional functions**

Detection	Analysis	Containment	Eradication	Recovery
• Monitor and identify signs for irregularity • Collect information and intelligence • Rule out false alarms • Escalate to security managerial functions and to analysis • Start preserving logs relevant to the event and to the organizationl response	• Map impact on systems and data • Analyze attack vectors and their nature • Classify and prioritize the incident (triage) • Analyze the impacts on processes and services • Check third-party vulnerabilities • Forensic investigation • **Do not attack back the attacker** – finding who did it is the responsibility of State bodies	• Carefully isolate compromised system/s • Disable remote login and Disconnect problematic privileges • Block related processes • Use backups carefully • Try to neutralize the "weapons" of the attack (malware, backdoors, etc.) • Mitigate damages caused to organizational assets by the attack	• Fully block attackers' access to systems and data • Remove all attack components in systems and data • Fix damages caused to systems and data	• Restore from backups and restore corrupted data • Clean up invalid accounts and privileges • Validate the functionality and health of systems, processes and services • Perform risk assessment prior to "back to normal" • Return systems to full activity
------------- At this stage or after further analysis: • inform the CMT manager, activate the CSIRT, call external support professionals	------------- Until the end of the event: • Continuosly update and report to the CMT manager and other relevant parties			------------- Participate in lesson learned activities and, accordingly, improve Cyber security means and processes

Ransom demands -

Ransomware is a type of malware that prevents or limits users from accessing their system, either by locking the system's screen or by locking the users' files unless a ransom is paid.

More modern ransomware families, collectively categorized as crypto-ransomware, encrypt certain file types on infected systems and forces users to pay the ransom through certain online payment methods to get a decrypt key.

In certain cases, ransom demands may arrive in other ways, such as an email message (from an unknown source).

As a general rule, immediately inform the Police or the National/Sectoral CERT, before paying the ransom !

Reporting to customers -

Cyberattacks on the organization's systems may have significant implications for customers – due to damaged or inaccessible data, loss of services or money theft.

Many organizations tend to keep cyberattacks in secret, as long as customers do not feel anything, or publish something like "we're currently experiencing some problems with our IT network", in case there are some disruptions in services.

It should be emphasized that international regulation is increasingly inclined to require reporting to customers and other external stakeholders about significant Cyber events and their implications.

Reporting obligations are also derived from the sector to which the organization belongs and the regulation relevant to this sector.

Media and Public Relations -

In times of crisis, the media and social media play a central role in shaping the organization's image and the public and customers confidence.

In view of the sensitivity that is sometimes associated with cyberattacks, the following aspects should be considered:

- Timing for exposing the incident
- Level of details of the information delivered to the public
- Coordination of messages with the relevant authorities (the regulator, law enforcement authorities, National CERT)

While approaching the media, the following should be ensured:

- Clear and simple messages
- "Unity of messages" in all the channels in which they are transferred
- Determination of the right "presenter" – i.e. the senior executive appearing in the media

Legal aspects -

Cyber events may have significant legal aspects, and therefore the involvement of legal counsel is required. The legal aspects may include:

- Compliance with legal and regulatory Cyber-related requirements
- Compliance with legal obligations to customers and other stakeholders
- Preservation of evidence
- Definition of the Cyber Forensics' boundaries
- Legal aspects related to ransom demands or other demands of attackers
- Coping with lawsuits
- Involvement in insurance matters (Cyber insurance and other relevant insurances related to the event)

Support from external sources -

The management of the crisis is the responsibility of the organization being attacked and its management.
However, companies and organizations can be assisted by external professionals while coping with Cyber incidents and crises.
The services offered take various forms, including:

- **Technological consultants** - assist the organization's professional staff in dealing with the incident and its technological implications
- **External Incident Response Teams (IRs)** - provide technological assistance on various aspects during an incident with a more holistic approach.
- **Experts in non-technological aspects** - for example, PR experts, Legal advice, or negotiation experts (to assist in the negotiation with the attackers)

At the same time, companies and organizations can, and sometimes even must, report, consult, and/or be assisted by state authorities during a significant Cyber incident.

These authorities include:

- The relevant regulator (if there is such a relevant regulator) - in accordance with existing regulations
- The national CERT
- Police - in situations where criminal activity is suspected

Cyber Crisis Management - General Organizational Setup -

Given all the aspects described above, the general organizational setup during a Cyber crisis looks like this:

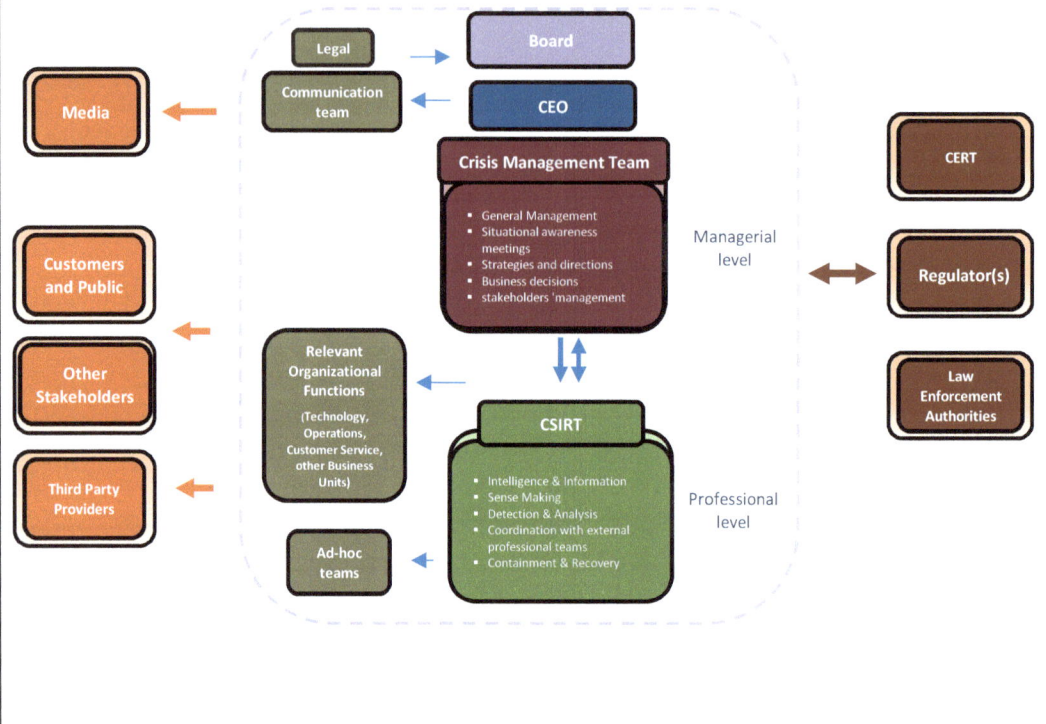

Cyber Crisis Management - General Organizational Setup

5. Situation Snapshot / Situation Assessment

The importance of information during a crisis -

Under conditions of uncertainty during a crisis there is usually a considerable lack of available and reliable information about what is happening, and the information obtained is often partial and even contradictory.

The standard sources of information are also insufficient, and therefore special arrangements are required.

Sources of information during a crisis

Under conditions of uncertainty during a crisis standard information sources are not sufficient - and therefore additional sources become essential

| Media | | International sources |

- Reliable information is not only important for effective decision-making, but it also reduces uncertainties in the organization and among stakeholders
- Information deepens trust and strengthens collaborations

Intelligence

| Employees as sensors | Customers | Systems | Authorities |

Efficient use of information sources requires the implementation of structured information gathering and information sharing processes in parallel to open mindedness and creative thinking

Situation Snapshot -	**Situation Assessment** -
A structured presentation of the available information at a given time regarding a particular reality or situation. The purpose of the Situation Snapshot in a Cyber crisis is to efficiently arrange the relevant information regarding the cyberattack(s) and its (their) impacts. The Snapshot needs to present information about: - The technological aspects of the incident - The relevant organizational, operational, business and reputational impacts	A systematic evaluation of a particular reality or situation, based on the Situation Snapshot and aimed at (1) understanding the key elements of the reality or situation (sense making), and (2) deciding how to respond or act *vis-a-vis* this reality or situation. **The purpose of the Situation Assessment in a Cyber crisis (or any crisis for that matter) is to make decisions regarding the required course of action**.

Basic format for a Situation Snapshot -

Snapshot of the Cyberattack   as of:

| Office 365 | ✉ ▲ | Outlook Calendar People Yammer OneDrive Sites Tasks |

Topics	Key Points	Actions (taken/planned)
Time of attack		
The attacker (as far as is known)		
Type of attack (vectors)		
Status of the attack + estimations for the next hours/days		
Attack Targets (Systems, infrastructure, databases)		
Assets penetrated / damaged		
Leaked or damaged data		
Impacts on services and processes (including potential impacts)		
Impacts on functional continuity		
Impacts on customers and other stakeholders		
Publication and publicity (regarding the incident)		
Contacts with authorities and external bodies		
Attackers' demands		
Required resources for coping with the attack (consultants, means, budgets)		

Snapshot Highlights		
Intensity of the Attack	**3.5**	
	Complexity of the attack	4
	Criticality of the asset being attacked	3
Severity of Impacts	**3.0**	
	Functional continuity	2
	Disruption of services to customers	2
	Data leakage	4
	Reputation	3

Situation Assessment meeting -

Participants:

- The Crisis Management team, the CSIRT manager

Invitees:

- Key professionals from relevant units

Agenda:

1 **Updates and clarifications**

- Presentation of the updated Situation snapshot by the CSIRT manager
- Additional information on essential issues - relevant managers, PR and legal counsel

2 **Decision making**

- Presentation of the required decisions and the main alternatives
- Focused discussion on the alternatives
- Making decisions about the course of action

3

- A quick summary of the decisions
- Distribution of tasks to the relevant parties

Guiding principles for the Situation Assessment meeting

- The meeting should be concise and purposeful
- The format of the meeting and the format of the Snapshot should be predefined
- The focus of the meeting needs to be on changes that have occurred since the previous meeting (not to start everything from the beginning)
- In order to make the meeting efficient, the Snapshot must be coordinated with all relevant parties before the meeting

6. Recovery and Return to Routine Operation

Recovery and Return to Routine Operation -

The decision to return to routine operation is under the responsibility of the CEO / Crisis Management Team manager and needs to be in accordance with relevant authorities' notifications.

Recovery actions may include:

- Conducting Risk Assessment towards returning to routine operations
- Completion of tasks and closure of processes that began during the crisis and are still in progress
- Removing vulnerabilities and installing or updating routers and firewalls to prevent unauthorized access
- Reinstalling clean versions
- Installing updated security patches
- Changing of passwords

- Generation of new access keys/authorizations
- Cleaning and deleting obsolete accounts and authorizations
- Deleting/amending disrupted / leaked data
- Restoring required data from backups
- Conducting a vulnerability scan of the compromised machine/system before reconnecting to the network
- Confirming the integrity of business processes and controls
- Notification to customers and other stakeholders on the return to routine operation, as applicable
- Notification to all relevant managers and employees that the organization is ready to return to routine operation

Documentation -

Documentation is needed for potential investigations and for lessons learned. It may include:

- A summary of the incident
- Major occurrences in a timeline format
- Indicators related to the attack's vectors and affected components
- Impacts on systems and data
- Logs and print screens related to the attack
- Actions taken by all incident handlers on this incident
- Contacted/involved external parties
- Comments from incident handlers

Lessons Learned -

The lessons learned process after an incident should refer, among other things, to the following:

- Information / intelligence prior to the event
- The escalation mechanisms and the activation of the response plan
- The CSIRT activity
- Coping with the malware
- Use of external consultants / experts
- Coordination with the various business units
- Crisis Management Team's activity
- Coping with the media
- Coordination with the national / sectoral authorities
- Information sharing with other organizations
- Supporting means and tools
- Human resources aspects (quantity, skills)

Preparedness - Main building blocks -

- Professional knowledge of the Cyber security staff
- General awareness among employees and managers
- Technological Simulations
- Managerial exercises (at all levels)

- Cyber Security policy
- Cyber Security Governance (responsibilities)
- Cyber Incident Response plan
- Procedures and supporting managerial tools for incident management

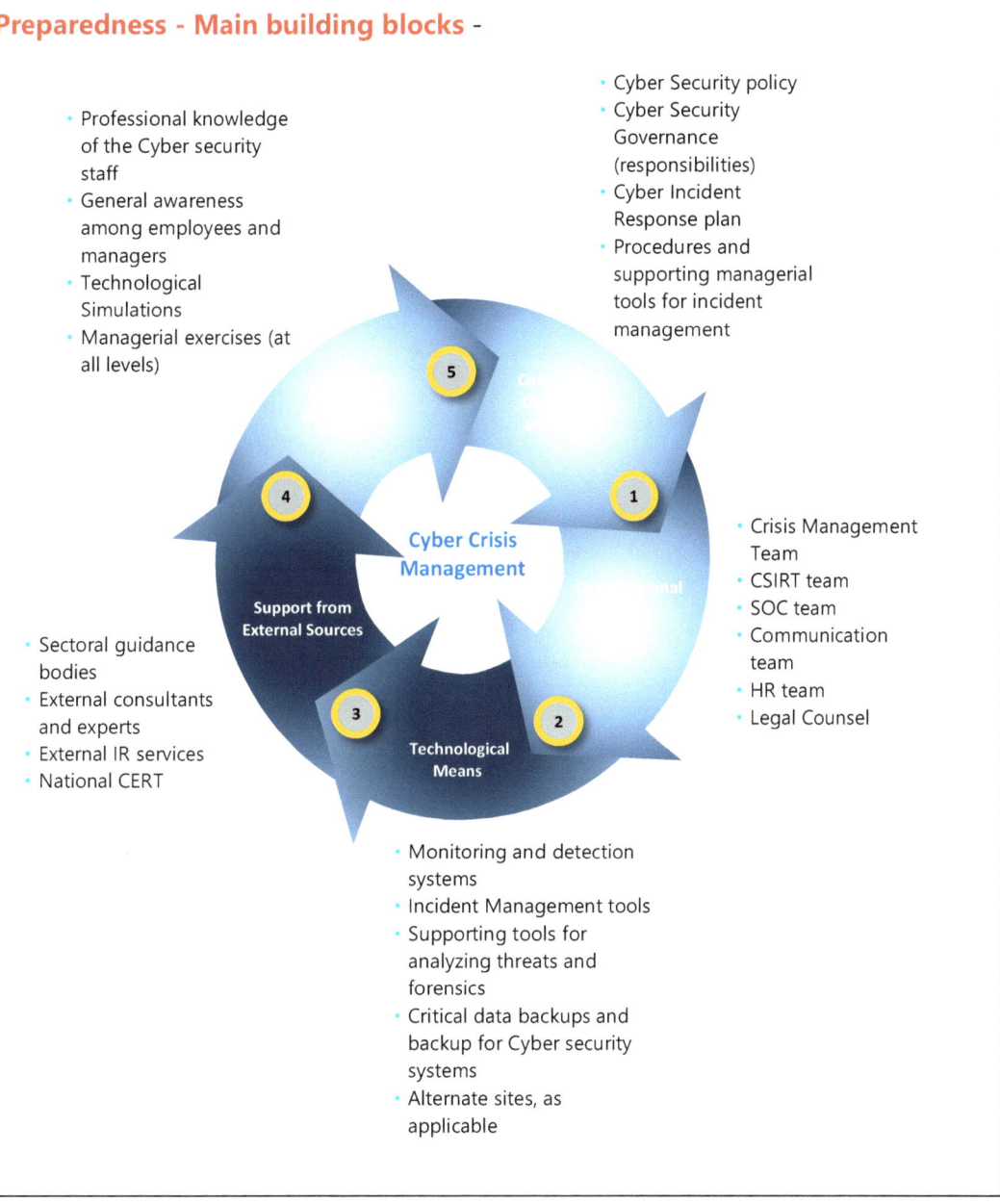

- Crisis Management Team
- CSIRT team
- SOC team
- Communication team
- HR team
- Legal Counsel

- Sectoral guidance bodies
- External consultants and experts
- External IR services
- National CERT

- Monitoring and detection systems
- Incident Management tools
- Supporting tools for analyzing threats and forensics
- Critical data backups and backup for Cyber security systems
- Alternate sites, as applicable

Organizational Cyber Security Policy ("Policy" document) -

The purpose of the Policy document is to outline an overall approach for organizational preparedness in the field of Cyber Security - both during routine times and while coping with a significant Cyber incident or crisis.

The Policy outlines guiding principles, from which the operational plans and specific Cyber Security procedures are derived.

Among other things, the organizational **Policy should include reference to the following:**

- The guiding regulation
- Organizational goals with respect to Cyber Security
- Threats and Reference Scenarios
- The general framework for Cyber Security Risk Management

- The organizational Governance with respect to Cyber Security (responsibilities)
- Information Security policy
- The Concept of Operation during significant Cyber incidents and crises
- Service levels and recovery objectives
- Cyber Incident Severity Levels
- Support from external sources in the event of a significant Cyber incident
- Interfaces with external authorities
- Critical assets and processes
- Critical suppliers
- Means for protection, monitoring and control
- Awareness, training and exercises

Risk Management -

The role of the CRO and the Risk Management functions is to lead the formulation of a suitable Cyber Security Risk Management framework and to challenge organizational policies, plans, procedures and controls.

Periodic risk assessments and risk mitigations with respects to Cyber Security should be conducted.

Complex Risk Assessment methodologies do not necessarily bring better results.

Cyber Security Risk Map -

Compliance
- Compliance wih the law
- Compliance with regulation
- Compliance with binding international standards
- Internal and external audits

Organizational Precept
- Organizational Cyber Security Policy
- Cyber Security Governance
- Framework for Risk Management
- Cybersecurity and Information Security procedures

Access Control
- Identity Management
- Authorizations and passwords
- Encryption
- Separation of environments
- Monitoring and intrusion control systems

Security Configuration
- Cyber Asset Management
- Anti-virus systems
- Databases security
- Networks security
- Applications security
- Digital services security
- Securing sensitive services
- Remote access security
- Workstations and servers
- Portable devices - BYOD

Third Party
- Supply chain procedures
- Outsourcing
- Cloud services

Readiness for Incidents
- SOC and its procedures
- Data backups and systems backup
- Incident Response plan
- Cyber Crisis Management plan
- External IR support
- Supporting tools for Incident Response

Threats and Vulnerabilities
- Threat assessments and Reference Scenarios
- Vulnerability Scans
- Penetration Tests

Physical Security
- Entrance controls
- Security measures at sites and facilities

Awareness and Training
- General awareness among employees and managers
- Professional skills of the technological staff
- Simulations and Exercises

Awareness and Training -

Trainings should be carried out periodically in the organization - in order to raise general awareness to Cyber security, to ensure an adequate professional level among the professional staff, and to maintain suitable competence of the teams responsible for managing significant Cyber incidents and crises.

Target populations for Cyber Security trainings

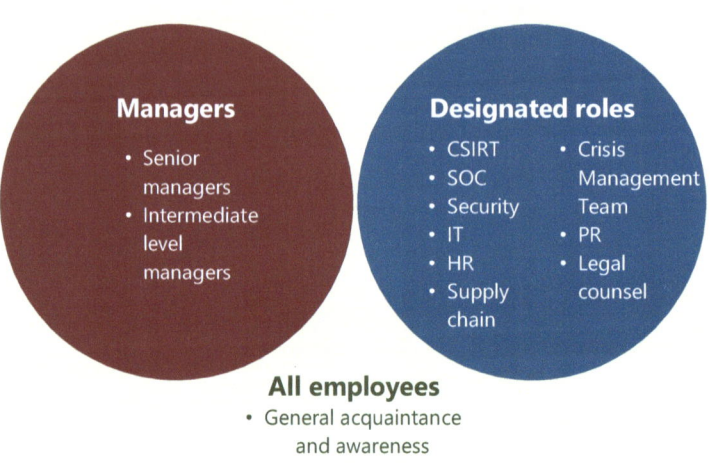

Managers
- Senior managers
- Intermediate level managers

Designated roles
- CSIRT
- SOC
- Security
- IT
- HR
- Supply chain
- Crisis Management Team
- PR
- Legal counsel

All employees
- General acquaintance and awareness

Simulations and exercises -

Simulations and exercises are the best tools for assimilating Cyber Security awareness, developing familiarity with the response plans (and at same time challenging these plans), and encouraging lessons learned and improvement.

It is recommended to set a two-year exercising program for the various simulations and exercises.

Exercises can consist of different scopes and participating populations - technological teams, managers, representatives from the entire organization - and can be carried out by various methods:

- Simulations of technological events in systems

- Table Top exercises

- Comprehensive managerial exercises

Table Top exercises -

Round Table

- Examining alternatives and making decisions in the framework of a joint meeting (in the same room)
- Suitable for relatively small groups of practitioners

Functional Teams

- A more dynamic exercise format that integrates team thinking and plenary discussions

Large Scale Cyber Security managerial exercise -

- **Our unique experience**
- Operation, Cyber and business challenges
- Senior management and **dozens** of other participants from all units
- Vertical and horizontal information flow
- Simulation of stakeholders: staff, customers, media, regulators, suppliers, the general public, etc.
- Decision making processes under pressure

A very dynamic and multidisciplinary exercise

In practice it looks like this:

IT Team

Control Team

Me

Request from CEO
Subject: Immediate Wire Transfer

To: Chief Financial Officer
High Importance
Please process a wire transfer payment in the
amount of $250,000 and code to "admin expenses"
by COB today. Wiring instructions below.

Crisis Management Team

Press Conference

Communication Team

Dr. Ishai Dror, Israel
ishaid20@gmail.com

www.ingramcontent.com/pod-product-compliance
Lightning Source LLC
Chambersburg PA
CBHW041319180526
45172CB00004B/1154